Little

PRESIDENT

TRUMP'S

SANDBOX

I0624299

DELAWARE

DEDICATED TO

For all our children
like Michael, Andrew, Gail, and Alicia.

GOD, COUNTRY, FAMILY, FRIENDS.

THE BLACK DIAMOND EFFECT® ....Volume 1, No. 2
LITTLE PRESIDENT TRUMP'S SANDBOX (DIGEST EDITION)

The sky was clear
on this bright sunny day.

Little President Trump had great plans to convey.

GEORGIA

With shovels and buckets he'd lead the way,
and make the sandbox a great place to play.

CONNECTICUT

Little President Trump, he puffed out his chest
and declared that this sandbox could still be the best.

With a confident grin and a plan on display
he was eager to tell the whole world of his way.

MASSACHUSETTS

So he set out with all of the might he could muster and garnered the aid of each new little tusker.

"To get every task done, I'll need elephants grand, to move and reshape this great big box of sand!"

NEW HAMPSHIRE

The dream of the sandbox
was that all kids were equal.

"Things have to be fair,
and I know my technique will
make sure that each kid in
the box has their shot
to play and to learn with
the toys that they brought."

VIRGINIA

"The rules of the sandbox have got to be just, and enforced by good people that everyone trusts."

NORTH CAROLINA

"So I'll put in some judges to see that the rules are followed by all, at work and at schools."

RHODE ISLAND

"And speaking of schools,
that's a system that's broken.
On this, I'm aware,
that I'm very outspoken."

VERMONT

"There's a reason this topic has made me so vocal:
To fix education, we must keep it local!"

KENTUCKY

All the work to be done would require lots of spark.
It just wouldn't do to be stuck in the dark.

"We need energy, lots of it, to help meet our goal.
We'll need wind, we'll need water.
We'll need solar and coal!"

TENNESSEE

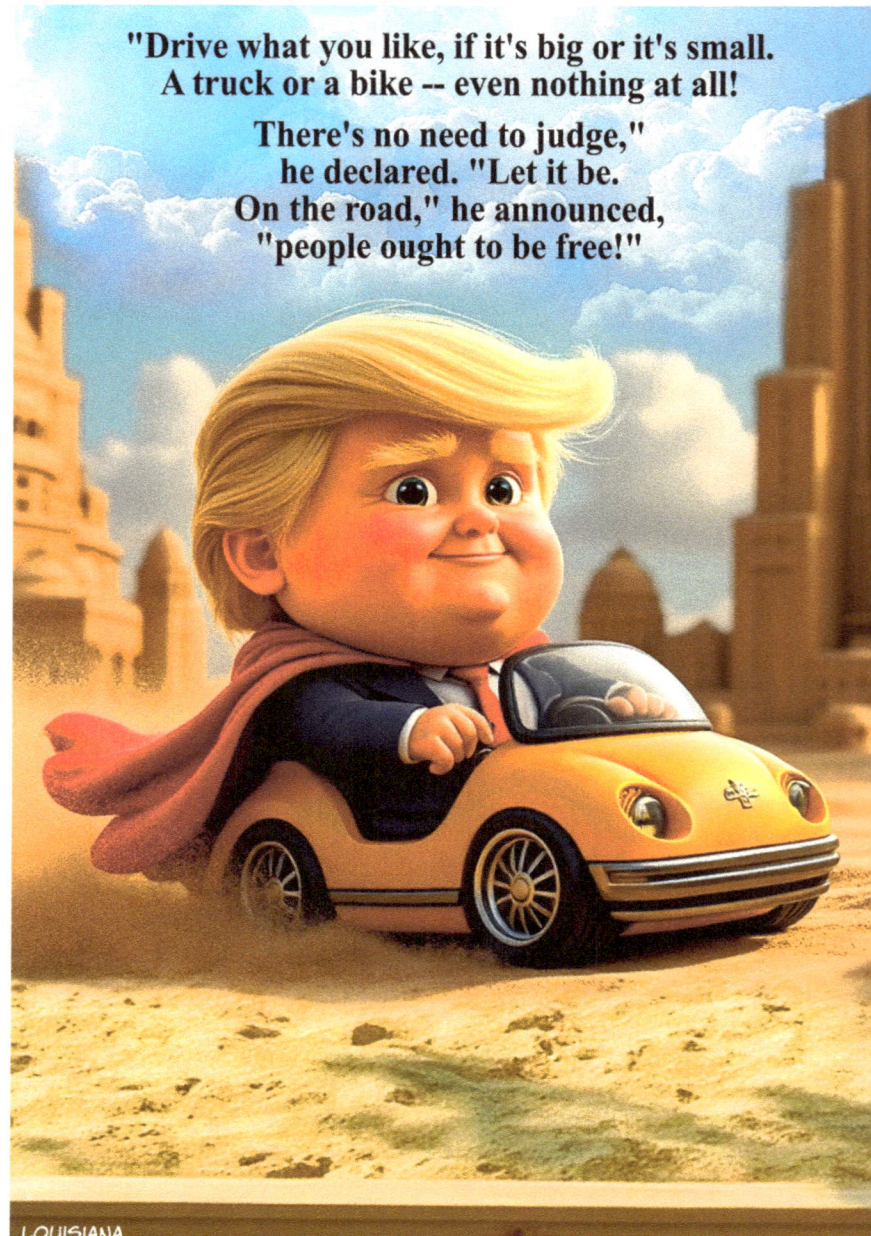

But those cars require fuel to get them where they go.
Little President Trump nodded and said, "Yes, I know.
That means we need oil if their tanks we will fill."

Then he grinned a sly grin, and said, "Drill, baby, drill!"

INDIANA

"So I'll take all that knowledge,
the big and the small.
And I'll use it to make everyone safe --
with a wall!"

ILLINOIS

Growing up in New York, he had lots of good treats.
like a pizza all covered with cheeses and meats!

And like every New Yorker,
he knew a good piece
would be wide and be thin,
and be dripping with grease.

ALABAMA

He liked other foods, too.
He wasn't too picky.
He liked foods that were dry.
He liked foods that were sticky.

And he liked most to share it.
He did that with ease.
He would sit with the team and
have burgers with cheese.

The best part of the sandbox -- it was all outdoors.
Little President Trump thought it would attract tours.

"I want to protect outdoor places this great!"
So he made a new rule, with no room for debate.

MICHIGAN

"Don't be mean to your pets,
that's a bad thing to do!
Your animal friends are all counting on you."

"Feed them and love them, each kitty and pup!
And when they make messes,
get a scoop and clean up!"

FLORIDA

In his sandbox he made every one get along.
He wouldn't be bullied. You couldn't do wrong.

When he played in the sand, everybody knew peace.
Fighting all over the playground would cease.

But that didn't mean everyone had to agree.
These were laws,
but they weren't made by royal decree.

"In this sandbox, everyone gets to write or to say anything that they want. That's the American way!"

WISCONSIN

Even the birds, with their cheeping and chirping,
get to say what they will, be it hiccups or burping!

"We can share our ideas, whether simple or complex."
And he signed off this statement with a big letter X.

Everyone wanted to play in the sand.
But the box wasn't made to be so over-ran.

So Little President Trump
drew a line with some chalks.
"If we don't have a border,
we don't have a box!"

OREGON

The box had its rules, but he was only one kid.
He couldn't watch over everything others did.

So he supported his friends
with their blue hat and shirt,
who made sure kids played safely,
without getting hurt.

KANSAS

"If someone gets hurt, I need someone who's brave
to rush to the scene and the day then to save."

And the bravest became
Little President Trump's friends
on whose courage every one in the sandbox depends.

WEST VIRGINIA

"But I'm just a Little President -- I'm not an M.D.
So I'll make sure everyone has good doctors to see."

NEBRASKA

Little President Trump set his eyes on the stars.
"One day," he said, "we will put men on Mars."

"We'll go even further,
and so I'll endorse
A new branch of the military.
We'll call it Space Force!"

COLORADO

And so with a vision of strength and resolve
Little President Trump's plan began to evolve.

Some people, they laughed, and said, "It won't fly!"
Now the sandbox is guarded from way up in the sky.

NORTH DAKOTA

In another sandbox that was far, far away
there were soldiers who fought
to keep bad guys at bay.

But the foes were all stopped,
so he said, "Come on back
to our sandbox at home,
where there's no more attack."

WASHINGTON

Little President Trump held a sincere regard
for the brave folks who kept the sandbox under guard.

He saluted them all as he surveyed the land,
with a grin on his face and a flag in his hand.

"These folks are the bravest,
the brightest and best!

They've fought every fight and
they've passed every test!"

WYOMING

"I'm proud that our sandbox has got the best team!"

And as one, they stood tall -- and their eyes held a gleam.

Little President Trump did the best he could do
so the sandbox was a place
all folks could look up to.

OKLAHOMA

And all who played in it gave a cheer,
and a jump:
"Hip Hip Hooray for Little President Trump!"

NEW MEXICO

Little President Trump had fun all that day
making his sandbox a great place to play.

He built and he dug, with a smile so wide,
but soon it was time to go back inside.

So he waved goodbye. It was time to adjourn
so others could get in the sand for their turn.

He'd done all he could --
but this wasn't the end...

ALASKA

...and he just couldn't wait to go do it again.

HAWAII

www.ingramcontent.com/pod-product-compliance
Lightning Source LLC
Chambersburg PA
CBHW051558120626
46551CB00013B/1577